# WASTE FREE KITCHEN

*Save Money, Stay Organized & Reduce Waste*

## KATE ANDERSON

© 2015

# Table Of Contents

# Introduction: A Waste Free Kitchen!

For most households, the kitchen is the center of our homes. It's where we eat, where we converse, where we get creative, where we make plans, where we entertain, and often it's even where we work! If your home is like my home, you'll agree that there's always life in the kitchen. Either the kids are at the table doing their homework, my husband and I are chatting over tea, stacks of bills and papers are lying around waiting to be paid or organized, or our extended family and friends are visiting. With all this hustle and bustle, it can be hard to keep our kitchens tidy, let alone organized! What's worse is how much time, energy, and money we actually spend on keeping this one room in action!

In this simple guide, I offer tons of bright ideas to help you get organized and save money. I will show you all the best tricks to declutter your kitchen counters, keep your family organized, reduce waste, and get the most out of your grocery shopping so you can be sure to keep your pockets (and your stomachs!) full! And not only that, but I will also provide you with some clever kitchen hacks and offer you some of my own favorite money-saving recipes that your family are sure to love!

# Part One: Getting Organized and Reducing Waste

The kitchen has often been called the "brain" of the household. It's usually the place we keep all that stuff we need but don't know exactly where it belongs! That means most of us have at least one "junk drawer", at least one pile of random papers, all kinds of hidden food ingredients lurking at the back of our cupboards, an ironically messy cleaning cupboard, and a variety of other disorganized and untidy corners and countertops. You'll be happy to know that keeping your kitchen organized is a lot easier than you think! You don't have to be a "clean freak" in order to get tidy!

No matter how small your kitchen is or how many people live in your household, the following list will show you how you can transform any messy or unorganized kitchen into the sleek and highly functioning kitchen of your dreams!

# 7 Ways to Organize Your Cupboards and Drawers

## 1.) Start With A List

Before you go out and buy tons of plastic containers, baskets, and accordion files, make a list of which cupboards need your attention. Is your refrigerator a disaster? Is your junk drawer overflowing? Do your plastic food containers come tumbling out every time you open the cupboard door? Make a list of what needs done and tackle your cupboards one at a time.

There are a number of things you will want to group together into categories (arts and crafts materials, first aid supplies, eating utensils, tin foil and plastic wraps, herbs and spices, etc.). Write a list of how many categories you have and what types of tubs or baskets you will need. Think about the space you have available and what type of boxes will work best for your needs. For instance, if you only have space for small tubs or baskets, don't go out and buy large cumbersome ones! Or, if you only have a few arts and crafts supplies, you might be better off including them in your stationery box or storing them with you kitchen wraps and freezer bags rather than dedicating a whole box for art supplies!

The important thing is to make sure everything has a place. That's the most important thing about being organized! Remember that you don't necessarily have to *buy* anything. You can re-use shoe boxes, wicker or wire baskets, plastic food containers, rubber bands, glass jars, and/or any other receptacles you might have lying around! For a sleeker looking kitchen, use baskets/tubs that match.

## 2.) Make Sure Everything Has A Place

The most important part of organizing a kitchen is making sure everything has a place. Most kitchens have a cupboard for pots and pans, cutlery, plates and bowls, and glassware. But what about all that junk mail and your bills? What about your children's art projects? Is there an unsightly pile of random papers taking up space on your countertops?

Reclaim your countertops by making sure everything has a place. Use tubs, baskets, and jars to tidy things into categories. Make sure to put a label on everything to keep the whole household on board! Use a ring binder to keep your bills and papers organized. Throw away anything that is old or unnecessary. If you have old magazines or newspapers lying around, get rid of them. If there are articles you want to save, cut them out, store the clippings in a specific place, and throw the rest away.

Display your children's artwork in frames or on the fridge. Save any other special things in file blocks or in lidded containers at the top of your closet or in another unused space. Make sure you aren't keeping things that you will never look at again. When saving your children's school work, make a rule to only save those things you will later enjoy looking through. Unless this week's math homework is a work of academic or comedic genius, throw it out! Take time to regularly move older kid stuff into the attic or garage.

Once you're sure everything has a place, don't forget to *USE IT*!


## 3.) Go Paperless

If you really want to tackle a stack (or closet full) of papers, go paperless! Take photos of your important papers and get rid of them. Nowadays, most telephone, internet, and electricity suppliers offer invoices via email. Most banks and credit card companies offer statements and credit card bills via email as well. Sign up to use these services and you'll not only save space and stay organized, but you'll also reduce waste!


## 4.) Label Everything

Sometimes we have the best intensions of keeping things organized and tidy but we lose our way or other people sharing our household don't follow suit. To keep everyone in your home on board, label all baskets, jars, tubs, and other containers to keep everyone on the same page. This way you won't have to clean up after everyone!


## 5.) Use the Insides of Cupboard Doors

You'd be surprised how handy the doors on your cupboards can be! If you keep your cleaning products in a cupboard under the sink, you might be constantly frustrated searching for sponges, brushes, and rubber gloves. Why not hang a fabric pocket organizer on the inside of the cupboard for your bits and pieces? You could even make one yourself with unused fabrics, or old sheets or towels!

Another great thing you can use your cupboard doors for is reminders and schedules. You can hang a cork notice board or a blackboard on the back of a cupboard door for to-do lists, homework schedules, family chore tasks, telephone messages, or other family reminders!

## 6.) Use Your Space Wisely

This is a great tip for people with small kitchens or limited storage space. In order to use your space wisely think outside the box. Do you have space on the top of your cupboards that isn't being used? Why not store some stuff in boxes or homemade pull-out drawers up there? Do you have a cupboard that could be used better? For instance, are your pots and pans stacked neatly or could you organize them better to buy yourself some space to store other things in the same cupboard? Most importantly, are your cupboards full of things you don't need or use? Get rid of anything you don't need. Then put anything you don't use regularly in a high up space, in another room, or at the back of a cupboard. Keep the things you need regularly in the most accessible places. This will buy you more space and you won't waste time looking for your favorite pots and pans amidst your specialty baking supplies or that juicer you used once!

## 7.) Get Rid Of Unnecessary Clutter

Most people have at least a few things they could get rid of. You might have 4 whisks that are all identical or 3 small pots when you only ever use one. You might still have parts for an old broken food processor. You might have dried foods or ingredients that are out of date. What about that box of crackers that's been open for 6 months? Get rid of it! Or those half used birthday candles from 5 years ago? Toss them out!

Go through your kitchen and decide which things you really need and which things you could do without. Be ruthless. If you are prone to holding on to things that aren't necessary, get a friend over to encourage you to let go.

If you have unused and unwanted canned goods or dried foods that are still in date, give them to a friend or donate them to a local charity or food drive. If you have an old tea set that you never use anymore, sell it online or have a yard sale. If you no longer need that second set of cutlery or that old blender, offer it to a friend or relative that might find a use for it. If you can't find a use for something at all, throw it away!

Once you've got your kitchen nicely organized and everything has a place, use this next list to learn how to save money and be kind to the environment by reducing waste. This list will show you some inventive ways to turn your trash into treasure!

# 5 Ways To Reduce Waste Fast!

## 1.) Re-use Jars And Containers

Think of everything you purchase as having a future purpose. Save glass jars from jams and sauces as storage for pasta, rice, dried beans, homemade granola, snack mix, or candle holders! Keep your take-away containers for your own leftovers or drawer organizers. Keep your empty spray bottles from kitchen cleaners and use them for new homemade cleaners.

*Top Tip: To remove stubborn labels from glass jars, combine 1 part coconut oil and 1 part baking soda. Saturate the label with the mixture, leave to rest for an hour, and then peel off. Scrub excess glue off with a scouring sponge.*

## 2.) Keep Perishables At The Front Of Your Cupboards

In order to get the most out of your fresh foods, always store them at the front of your refrigerator and cupboards so you remember to use them before they go out of date. Keep your dried and canned goods at the back. This means you'll use all your fresh breads, fruits, and veggies instead of letting them go to waste. This is a great way to save money and get the most out of your groceries.

## 3.) Keep It Airtight

Keep all foods you don't use very often fresh and safe. Store flour, sugar, dried fruit, nuts, cereals, and other dried goods in airtight containers or freezer bags. This will keep them fresh and safe from unwanted house guests like bugs and mice.

## 4.) Think Twice Before You Throw It Out

There are a lot of things we regularly throw away that could be useful. You can reduce your waste and save money by reusing things you would normally throw out. Not only can you use jars and other lidded containers for food storage but almost any "trash" could be useful in the future. For instance, cereal boxes, tin foil, tissue paper, and paper towel rolls might be useful for arts and crafts projects like stenciling, modeling, or other school projects. Small plastic tubs from yogurts or pudding can be useful as paint pots. Plastic containers from things like berries or mushrooms can be used to grow herbs in. Rubber bands and string might also come in handy later! Remember, reusing things is great for the environment and could save you a lot of money in the future. Just remember to keep your materials organized and throw them away if you know you won't use them!

## 5.) Re-use Sandwich Bags

Now I'm not suggesting you re-use baggies that are full of old food remnants, but I am suggesting that sandwich bags might be worth re-using. For instance, if you stored something like pretzels or peanuts in a sandwich bag, you might still use that bag again for screws, nails, or arts and crafts supplies. Think outside the box! Before you throw something away, ask yourself if it might serve a purpose later.

Don't forget: This isn't an excuse to become a hoarder! If you can't re-use something throw it away or recycle where possible.

# Part Two: Saving Money!

Food and cleaning supplies can cost you a fortune, but the don't have to. The average American family throws away 25% of the food they purchase; an average of $1,500 per year! Statistics show families in the UK are about the same. This section will offer you everything you need to know to keep your costs down but giving you shopping tips, cleaning hacks, and some of my favorite money saving recipes. Get more bang for your buck by trying the tips in the following lists.

# 7 Tips For Smarter Shopping

1.) Plan Your Meals

One of the best things you can do to keep your grocery costs down is to plan ahead. Decide on 5 to 7 dinners you'll have time to cook throughout the week and put the ingredients on your shopping list. Always keep ingredients for one or two easy meals in your kitchen incase of very busy days or unexpected changes to your schedule to avoid spontaneous eating out! Write down what you will need for lunches and snacks for your whole family for the week. Use the same lunch and snack ingredients for the whole family where possible to avoid spending extra money buying different things for everyone.

Then when you are shopping, stick to your list! I cannot stress this enough. Do not get distracted by sales or other things you don't need or didn't budget for. Try not to allow every member of the family to come to the grocery store with you so you can make sure you only buy what's necessary.

*Top Tip: If you know you're particularly susceptible to sale shopping or you can't manage to get to the store without bringing your kids along, buy your groceries online so you can be sure you'll stick to your list.*

## 2.) Take Stock

Before you do your grocery shopping, take stock of what you already have in your kitchen. Check your perishables and your dried and canned goods. Check your cleaning supplies and toiletries. If you've taken stock, you will know what you have at home because your shopping list will reflect it. Now, instead of asking "Do we need bananas?", you will know that you don't because they're not on your list. That means you won't buy them "just in case" or just because they're on sale.

For the same reason, try not to pop into the grocery store without a list. Often when we're in the store, our eyes begin to wander and we might buy 10 things instead of the 3 things we popped in for!

## 3.) Be Smart About Sales

Grocery stores make a large portion of their profits by putting things on "sale". And that's because it's hard to say no to a good bargain! However, in-store offers might encourage you to spend money on products you don't need or which might go out of date before you get a chance to use them. Whenever you see something that's "buy one get one free" or "3 for 2" don't lose your head! Only take advantage of sales when you were already going to buy the product or when you can be sure it will not go to waste. For instance, take advantage of sales on paper products and dried or canned goods that you regularly use. Or cash in on sales on family favorites such as peanut butter, favorite cereals, or crackers, etc. Avoid sales on dairy, fruit, and vegetables unless they were already on your list. Always avoid special offers on snack foods and junk foods.

Getting sucked into these types of sales is a waste of your money. It's ok to allow yourself a small budget for junk food, but being fooled into buying more than you need might make you exceed it!

Also, if something on your list happens to be "3 for 2", make sure you actually need 3 before buying 3! If you only need one and you buy three, you're spending more money than necessary and you might end up throwing the extra 2 away.

*Top Tip: If you have plenty of room in your freezer, take advantage of sales on bread products you and your family love and freeze them for a later date!*

## 4.) Get A Few Meals Out Of One Ingredient

This rule is best when applied to fresh or perishable ingredients. Have you ever noticed that when you buy a bag of spinach, you use half of it and then let the rest of it go bad? A lot of refrigerators are full of half-used, rotting fruits, vegetables, cheeses, creams, and whatever else you can think of. Instead of letting the remaining parts of your specialty or perishable ingredients go bad, think ahead! When you are planning your meals for the week, don't choose 6 recipes that each require 20 different ingredients! If you do, your groceries are going to cost you a fortune and half of them will end up in the trash by next week. Rather, if you know you are going to buy a certain ingredient that and only use half of it for one meal, plan another meal around that ingredient.

For instance, if you're buying a butternut squash to make a spicy curry, use half of it for your curry on Monday and turn the rest of it into a soup on Tuesday (*and* pack it in your lunch box on Wednesday!). Or if you're planning on buying fresh mozzarella cheese for a Sunday lasagna and you expect to have some leftover, plan to make a pizza for a special Tuesday dinner or a salad caprice for Thursday lunch. What about that jar of pesto that's been sitting in the back of your fridge? It's probably ready to be thrown out now! But next time you buy pesto, make sure you're actually going to use all of it by planning a few meals around it!

## 5.) Use What's In Season

Guess what! Eating what's in season isn't just good for you and the environment, it's also good for your wallet! There are a number of reasons that "in season" produce is cheaper than, say, strawberries in January. I'll break it down for you in a three simple facts:

1. Local produce is almost always cheaper because it doesn't have to travel to get to you.

2. Produce that's in season is more likely to be locally sourced, and available to you without added packaging and travelling costs.

3. When produce is in season, there's more of it, so naturally it will be cheaper to buy!

So take advantage of the seasons and watch your grocery bills lighten up!

## 6.) Be Smart At The Farmer's Market

There's nothing better than a good farmer's market. There are so many tasty things to buy and you can get fresh local ingredients at decent prices. Markets can be a great way to support local businesses and they can be a nice way to spend a weekend morning with your family. However, sometimes we get swept up in the sights and smells and end up spending a lot more money than we expected. If you find yourself easily distracted by all the culinary delights at the market and you know you're likely to spend a lot of money there, save marketing for a special outing rather than trying to do your grocery shopping there.

The best way to make market shopping work for you is to attack it the same way you do with your other grocery shopping: make a list and stick to it! If your children are likely to cost you a fortune in soft pretzels and crepes, leave them at home! Alternatively, give yourself a budget and whatever you do, make sure you stick to it!

## 7.) Shop Around

Yes it seems obvious and maybe a bit old fashioned, but taking the time to source cheaper groceries could save you a bundle. Shopping around for deals might be too time consuming for some people but there are some simple ways you can achieve it. For one, listen to other people! If you hear someone talking about how cheap their breakfast cereal is, ask them where they got it! Keep your eyes out for sales online, in newspapers, or in shop windows. If you know you can get paper towels cheaper in a different store, next time you're in the neighborhood, stock up. Remember, the difference of a few pennies may not seem like much at the time, but over the course of a year, they could add up to substantial savings.

Now that you're shopping smarter, here's some ways you can cook smarter too! This next list will offer you some top cooking tips to save money and get more life out of your perishable foods.

# Money-Saving Cooking Tips

1.) Make Your Own

It's shocking how much money we spend on cooking sauces, stocks, salad dressing, baby food, and countless other pre-packaged and/or processed food item. The fact is, homemade food is cheaper, healthier, and easier to make than you might think. If you already know your way around the kitchen and you have plenty of favorite recipes, make some time to get cooking! Take an afternoon to make large batches of soups, stews, sauces, stocks, casseroles, or any other family favorites. Divide them into single portions, wrap and label them, and stick them in the freezer. This way when you've had a long day at work and you're considering "ordering in", you'll have plenty of easy meals you can pop in the oven or microwave without spending a penny. If you don't have an afternoon to set aside for cooking, don't worry! Any time you do cook dinner, just make extra. Feed yourself and your family and freeze the leftovers. You can even freeze your leftover take-away pizza!

If you're a self-proclaimed "bad cook", have no fear! At the end of this book I'm going to give you a few of my favorite simple recipes so you can save money without having to take a course in the culinary arts! These are things that absolutely anyone can make, no matter how little time or skill. I promise!

Another great way to learn recipes is to spend time with friends or family members that could show you a few things. Most people that are good in the kitchen are happy to share their tips and recipes. Just ask them!

2.) Get The Most Out Of Your Bread

Earlier, I urged you to go light on perishable items when shopping but sometimes, no matter how much we plan ahead, we just don't get around to eating all the fresh food we've bought. So what do you do with all those bread products you never got a chance to eat?

Depending on the size of your family and their appetite for bread, there are a number of ways to make sure you never throw your bread in the trash again. You can freeze a whole loaf of bread when it's close to its expiry date to stop it from going moldy. Or if you only use half a loaf of bread at a time, take out how much you need when you first buy it and freeze the rest. If you don't eat much bread at all, put the whole loaf in the freezer and just take a slice out when you need and defrost it in the toaster or toaster oven. The same goes for pancakes, waffles, bagels, or any other bread product!

*Top Tip: If you're freezing bagels, always cut them before you freeze them! That way you can put them straight in the toaster without having to wait for them to thaw.*

There are other things you can do with excess bread too. Make croutons for your salad! Make French toast and freeze it for a special midweek breakfast! Stick your bread in the food processor and make bread crumbs to use with your favorite recipes instead of spending money on the store bought stuff! This is also a great way to use the end slices of your loaf if you regularly throw them away. For extra flavor in your bread crumbs add some fresh or dried herbs like oregano, basil, or sage. Throw some sea salt and black pepper in there too. And of course, don't forget to freeze your bread crumbs until you need them.

## 3.) Get The Most Out Of Your Fruit

Stop letting your fruit go bad and throwing it away! If you have a lot of fruit that needs used quickly, the easiest thing to do is stick it in the blender and make smoothies, but there are other tricks as well. Most fruit can be frozen and used at a later date. To freeze berries or grapes, place them on a baking tray and put them in the freezer (this keeps them from getting stuck together). Once they're frozen, put them into an air tight freezer bag. The same method can be used for apple slices. Use your frozen fruit for smoothies or to liven up your pancakes or homemade muffins!

If it's bananas you have too many of, make banana bread or add a mashed banana into some pancake mix to add a natural sweetness to your breakfast. Alternatively, freeze your bananas whole and simply squeeze them out of their skin to use for baking or smoothies at a later date!

*Top Tip: Most berries and grapes are only in season during the summer months. Stock up at the end of the season while berries are still cheap and freeze them to use in autumn and winter.*

## 4.) Get The Most Out Of Your Vegetables

In order to get the most out of your veggies, start with the stuff you usually throw away. When you are prepping dinner take all of your trimmings (carrot peels, celery hearts, onion offcuts, herb stems etc.) and pop them in a freezer bag. Every time you prep, add your trimmings to that bag in the freezer. Use it later to make your own vegetable stock!

For other veggies that are close to expiration, make soup, baby food, or a delicious healthy juice so you get all the goodness before they go bad.  Alternatively, if you know you won't get a chance to use them, throw those veggies in that freezer bag of offcuts to buff up your homemade stock!

## 5.) Freeze Your Dairy Products

That's right, you heard me! Quite a few dairy products can be frozen, including milk! If you have a big enough freezer and you want to cash in on a supermarket sale on milk, go right ahead. You can freeze cheese too! If you have a block of cheese you won't use up in time, grate it and toss it in a spoonful of corn starch to keep it from clumping, spread it out on a baking sheet and stick it in the freezer. When it's frozen, sweep it into a freezer bag and use it for homemade pizza, lasagne, quesadillas, or a casserole. And what about those recipes that call for 1/3 of a cup of buttermilk? Am I the only one who buys buttermilk for that 1/3 of a cup and always ends up throwing away at least a pint of buttermilk afterwards? Since I learned buttermilk is freezable, you can be sure I won't be making that mistake again!

## 6.) Grow Your Own

Not everyone is lucky enough to have a big back yard or an allotment to grow all their own vegetables. But most people do have a window sill and that's all you need to grow your own herbs and even quite a few types of vegetables. Take a trip to your local garden supply store and look for seed packets of vegetables that are specifically easy to grow in containers, pots, and hanging baskets. There are a number of varieties of tomatoes, cucumbers, strawberries, and leafy greens that grow very well in "contained gardens".

One of my favorite things to grow is a salad box. You only need a small box or round container to grow your own salad. Buy a salad seed mix or mix your favorite types of salad greens for a tailor made salad box. I grow a few types of lettuce, peppery greens, baby spinach, and chard in mine. The best thing about growing salad is that you can use it pretty regularly because it keeps growing after you cut it! This means you could reduce your salad costs to nil.

Growing your own herbs is also simple and useful. Fresh herbs taste better in your cooking than dried ones and if you take good care of your plants, they could also keep your grocery costs down. Just remember to only keep herb plants that you'll actually use to make sure you use your time, space, and energy wisely.

*Top Tip: If your plants start to die or winter gets the best of them, cut and chop them and stick them in your freezer. Frozen herbs are a great addition to winter cooking.*

## 7.) Pack Your Lunches And Snacks

This is the oldest money saving trick in the book but packing your lunch really can save you money! If you do it right, that is. Many of us decide to pack our lunches to save money, but end up spending more money on pre-portioned packaging and "snack sized" packs of fruit, crackers, cheese, and countless other products designed to fit in your lunchbox. Unfortunately, packed lunches full of things like this rarely save you money. Instead of buying expensive products designed for your lunchbox, buy inexpensive products and pack them right.

Get the most out of your dinners by packing your leftovers for tomorrow's lunch. Buy a big bag of grapes at the start of your week. Wash them and bag them into five lunchbox size portions. Do them same with pretzels, cheese and crackers, and berries.

Next, make your own special snacks for the week. Grab a recipe for granola bars off a friend or the internet. Bake a batch on Sunday and pack them up for the week. Make up a nice mix of pretzels, nuts, and dried fruit to carry with you. If you tend to skip or buy breakfast, start packing some granola or homemade cereal to work with you. To get the most bang for your buck, use washable containers rather than spending a fortune on sandwich bags and food wraps.

## 8.) Get More Out Of Baking

There are a number of ways you can be more efficient with your baked goods, whether you bake all the time or once a year! The secret trick is… you guessed it: Freeze it! There are a number of ways you can use your freezer to your benefit when it comes to baked goods. Muffins, cookies, sweet breads, and cupcakes can all be frozen after baking. This is good news for all that banana bread you make with your over-ripe bananas! Simply wrap your baked goods, label them with the date, and freeze until the next time you're expecting company or you need something fun for your lunch box.

For cupcakes, freeze before icing them. Take them out of the freezer and let them thaw for a few hours or overnight. Then ice them in the morning. Having treats like this in your freezer is fantastic for those times your kids accidentally forget to tell you about a bake sale happening tomorrow!

When you're baking cookies, mix up a double batch and only bake how much you need. Take the remaining raw dough and press into a sausage shape. Wrap the dough with plastic wrap and stick it in the freezer. The next time you want to make cookies, avoid the time, energy, and mess by simply cutting your frozen dough into 1/2 inch slices and bake as usual.

## 9.) Take The Hassle Out Of Special Diets

In many households, there is someone who eats differently than the rest of the family. This may be because of an allergy or lifestyle choice or you may just have a picky eater on your hands. This is very common but not always easy to cater for. If you're making two meals every dinner time you're bound to feel under pressure. But not only that, you're probably spending more time and money than you need to too!

The first tip that will make things easier on you is to plan everyone's meals in advance. Before you go shopping and buy tons of ingredients that you *might* need, think about how you can get the most out of your ingredients by planning meals for your special dieter around the produce you're already purchasing for the rest of the family.

The second tip is plan to cook meals that will suit everyone. For instance, if you have a vegetarian in your home, make a vegetarian meal the whole household will enjoy 2 or 3 times per week so you only have to prepare one dish. If your special eater can't have gluten, use a gluten-free recipe for the whole family rather than wasting time and money making separate meals for everybody.
The third tip is use your freezer wisely! If there is someone in your home that eats differently all the time, make extra when you're cooking for them, divide the leftovers in individual portions and freeze them to make things easier on yourself at a later date.

10.) When There's "Nothing" To Eat

We're all guilty of this one (or if we're not, someone in our house is!). We say it when we don't feel like cooking. We say it when we'd rather order in. We say it when we genuinely can't figure out what to make because we're tired after a long day! So what's the answer when there's "nothing" to eat? Be prepared for times like these! Yes, it's important to have pre-portioned meals lined up in your freezer. But there are also a few other ways you can make sure there's always *something* to eat without heading to the grocery store for ingredients or making something from scratch when you really just want to sit down and relax.

        The best way to always be prepared is by always keeping your house stocked with some quick meals you and your family love. For some households this may be pasta with pesto (my simple pesto recipe is at the end of this book!), for others maybe grilled cheese sandwiches and tomato soup or maybe rice and beans (this recipe is also and the end of this book!). Some families love "breakfast dinners" when the house isn't stocked full of groceries. If that's your family, make sure you always have plenty of eggs in the house and a loaf of bread in the freezer. You can whisk up an omelette in less than three minutes and for under $5! What about french toast with some fresh berries and bananas? Or if pancakes are your poison, take this top tip: mix up the dry ingredients of a good pancake recipe and store it in a clip top jar or large freezer bag.

When there's "nothing" to eat in the house (or you fancy a quick indulgent breakfast), take out a few scoops of pancake mix, add milk and start flipping some flapjacks! If you're not entirely sure what I mean, don't worry, my 1-Minute Cinnamon Pancake recipe is also waiting for you at the end of this book.


Before I get to the recipes, this last list will show you some ways you can cut your cleaning costs down. Have you ever taken note of how much you spend on cleaning products per year? The average American family spends almost $700! I don't know about you, but that seems like an awful lot of money to keep my toilets and sinks clean. Check out these top tips that will keep your house spic and span without emptying your wallet!

# 7 Ways To Reduce Cleaning Costs

## 1.) Dish Soap: Not Just For Dishes!

You may not realise this but your dish soap is more valuable than it seems, yet it's cheaper than most specialty cleansers! Dish soap is extremely versatile. It's a fantastic stain remover for any type of stain on any type of fabric. This means you don't need to spend extra money on a special carpet cleaner or a magical laundry serum every time someone makes a mess. Keep an old toothbrush to hand and when a stain happens, get the dish soap out, brush it onto the stain, and let it do its magic. Then rinse and clean as usual. For best results hit stains with some soda water first and soak in cold water after dish soap treatment!

## 2.) Less Variety, Same Effectiveness

Ever noticed how certain cleaners are targeted specifically for your kitchen or your bathroom? Ever wondered why you can't use your kitchen cleaner in your bathroom? Guess what, you can! Most household cleaning cupboards contain far more variety than is necessary. You don't need a different cleaner for every single thing in your house. As a general rule, keep bathroom cleaners out of the kitchen in case of toxicity, but there's no reason your kitchen cleaners can't leave the kitchen! If in doubt, buy an all purpose spray the next time you're buying cleaning products rather than wasting money on two or more products that most likely contain the same ingredients.

## 3.) Use Vinegar

You would be surprised at how many uses there are for vinegar. Not only is vinegar non-toxic, it is outstandingly versatile! Instead of buying a special window cleaning spray, use vinegar and a scrunched up newspaper to do your windows. Put a couple teaspoons of vinegar in your washing machine to take out odours like sweat or urine. Clean and disinfect your coffee machine, microwave, refrigerator, and chopping boards with vinegar. Add a couple spoonfuls of vinegar to your dishwasher to leave your glasses streak-free and sparkling. You can even deter ants and fruit flies by leaving a small dish of cider vinegar out as a trap! Vinegar's miracle fixes are endless and cheaper than any store bought cleaner. Give it a try!

## 4.) Say No To Paper Towels

There are certain things that paper towels may be useful for, but the majority of household chores can be done with old towels and rags. Instead of getting rid of your towels when you want fluffy new ones, cut them into rags and use them to clean your house. You'll save a fortune on paper towels and you'll reduce waste. It's a win / win.

## 5.) Recycle Your Coffee Grounds

That's right! Stop throwing away your coffee grounds! Used coffee grounds have a variety of household and kitchen functions. First of all, they are great at absorbing food odours. Put a small dish of used coffee grounds in the back of your refrigerator instead of buying baking soda every time your fridge needs freshened up. Or use your coffee grounds on a sponge to remove grease from pots and pans, maple syrup spills from your kitchen counters, and dried on cereal milk from your dining table. If you have a garden, a back yard, or an outdoor container garden, sprinkle your used coffee grounds in and around your plants to fertilise them and keep bugs away.

## 6.) Make Your Own

The best way to save money on cleaning products and reduce waste is to make your own. And this doesn't have to stop at vinegar window treatments and dish soap stain removers! You can make simple all purpose cleaning sprays with lemon juice, vinegar, water, and baking soda! You can also use essential oils to save money in the long run and keep your cleaners non-toxic at the same time.

One of the easiest ways you can save money and reduce waste is to make your own laundry detergent. Store bought detergents aren't just expensive; they're also full of toxic chemicals that aren't good for the environment and might not be good for you and your family either. It's a lot easier than you think too! I've been making my own laundry detergent for years and I'd never go back to the store bought stuff. It costs a fortune! If making your own laundry detergent sounds like something you'd like to try out, check out some of my recipes in my book, "Natural Landry Detergent"!

## 7.) Just Use *Less*

The quickest and easiest way you can save money on cleaning products is to simply use less of them. When you are cleaning, use only as much as you *need* to actually clean something. You might be using twice as much toilet cleaner than is actually necessary. Or you might be using far more detergent than your laundry requires! The next time you're cleaning try using a little bit less of your cleaning products and see how the results are. If you need more, by all means use more. But test the waters by using less first. You might find that you only have to buy your cleaning products much less often this way

Now that you've learned how to organise your kitchen, reduce waste, shop smart and cook smart, it's time to move on to the fun stuff! Here are those recipes I promised you..

# Simple Recipes To Save You Time And Money

## Homemade Baby Food

Making your own baby food can save you a fortune as well as being much healthier for your little one. As you'll see here, baby food takes no time at all to prepare so there's really no reason not to!

Ingredients:
Any fruit or vegetable your baby likes and you have stocked up
Water

Some favourite combinations:
Apple, Carrot, and Cinnamon
Pear and Rhubarb
Butternut Squash and Carrot
Sweet Potato, Pumpkin, and Raisin
Peaches and Pears
Peas and Carrots

Method:
Cover your fruit and/or vegetables with water in a pot. Bring to a boil, and then simmer until soft. Remember not to add any salt or sugar to your recipes. Drain the water from the pot (but don't get rid of it!) and puree the cooked vegetables. For younger babies, puree until smooth and add some of the cooking water to thin it out for them. For older babies, leave it thick and allow small chunks when your baby is ready for them. After you've made your baby food, spoon it into ice cube trays and freeze (don't forget to label it with the date!). Later when you are ready to use it, simply pop out however many cubes you need, thaw and warm up in a pan or microwave.

Remember that when you boil fruit and vegetables, a lot of vitamins and nutrients end up in the water. To get the most out of your fruit and vegetables, use the water for things like baby rice, baby oatmeal, or chill it give it to your child as a drink on a hot day!

Baby food for a day out:
Take any of these things out with you when your on the go and simply mash them up with a fork when your baby gets hungry. Mix them together in different combinations to keep things exciting!

Mango
Banana
Avocado
Melon
Blueberries
Grapes
Nectarines
Peaches
Plums
Apples or Pears (microwave first and allow to cool)

*Top Tip: If you are introducing a new type of food to your baby, start by making a small batch. This way if he doesn't like it, you won't end up throwing too much away!*

# 1-Minute Cinnamon Pancakes

This is my personal favourite pancake recipe. In order to make pancakes in a minute, simply mix up a large batch of your dry ingredients (2 or 3 times the recipe below) and store it in a clip-top jar or freezer bag. When you want a special breakfast or snack, simply take out as much as you need, mix in the wet ingredients, and cook!

Ingredients (for 12 large pancakes):
Dry:
2 1/2 cups of plain (all-purpose) flour

2 tablespoons of sugar
2 teaspoons of baking soda
1 teaspoon cinnamon
1/2 teaspoon salt

Wet:
1 ripe mashed banana
2 cups milk
a small handful of fresh or frozen blueberries (optional)
low fat cooking spray (for cooking)

Method:
Combine ingredients and stir only until mixed through. Avoid over stirring! Heat a pan to medium heat and coat with cooking spray. Ladle pancake mix onto the pan and let sit until small bubbles appear at the surface (about 30 seconds to 1 minute), then flip and cook the other side. Remove from pan when pancakes are golden brown.

*Top Tip: Keep your pancakes in a low heated oven to keep them warm until you've cooked them all. Then your family can enjoy them all together!*

# Perfect Every Time Marinara Sauce

This sauce is simple to make and it's absolutely delicious. You will notice that I add a few unconventional ingredients like lentils and spinach to this sauce in order to "hide" some extra vitamins and nutrients in it (great if you have picky eaters in the house!). They make no difference to the taste at all but you can leave them out if you prefer.

I recommend making this sauce in large batches and freezing. Use it for pizza, spaghetti, lasagne, and any other dish you like! This recipe is for a large batch, simply cut it in half if you prefer to make less.

Ingredients:

2 tablespoons olive oil
4 cans of chopped tomatoes
1 can full of vegetable stock (measure in one of the empty tomato cans!)
4 cloves of garlic, minced
1 onion, finely chopped
6 "cubes" frozen spinach or a few handfuls of chopped, fresh spinach (optional)
1/2 cup of dry red lentils (optional)
1 whole celery stalk
1 whole carrot
3 teaspoons dried basil or 4 teaspoons chopped, fresh basil (or to taste)
1 1/2 teaspoons of dried oregano or 2 teaspoons chopped, fresh oregano (or to taste)
salt and pepper to taste

Method:
Heat the olive oil over medium/high heat in a large pot and add the onions. Allow them to sweat for a minute and then add the garlic and heat for 30 seconds. Then add the lentils and stir to coat them in the flavoured oil for 30 seconds to a minute. Next add the tomatoes, stock, and herbs. Place the carrot and celery stalk in whole. This is a great way to take some of the bitterness out of the tinned tomatoes! Bring the sauce to a simmer and allow to cook, uncovered, for 20 - 30 minutes, stirring regularly. When your sauce has reduced by about 1/3, remove it from the heat, remove the carrot and celery, and puree the sauce with a hand blender. You will notice that if you are using lentils, your sauce will be thick and "creamy".

## Rice and Beans

This recipe is fantastic when there's "nothing to eat" in the house. You can eat it on its own, topped with cheese and salsa with a side salad, or as a hearty filling for burritos or tacos. This recipe makes about 4 to 6 servings. I use brown rice here for added nutrients but if you prefer to cook with white rice, simply use 1 cup rice and 2 cups stock.

Ingredients:
1 tablespoon olive oil (or low fat cooking spray)
1 small onion, chopped
2 cloves garlic, minced
1 cup of brown rice
1 can black beans (or other favourite beans)
3 cups of vegetable stock
1 tablespoon tomato puree (or 1/2 can of chopped tomatoes)
2 teaspoons cumin
2 teaspoons fresh or dried coriander (cilantro)
1 teaspoon of ground coriander
1 teaspoon hot chilli powder (optional)

Method:
Heat the oil in the pan over medium/high heat. Add the onions, cook for one minute and then add garlic. Next add the rice, heat for 1 minute stirring constantly to coat it in the flavoured oil. Then add all remaining ingredients except the beans and stir. Bring to a boil, then reduce heat and simmer, covered, for 20 minutes. Finally stir in the beans and allow to cook for another 10 minutes. At this stage you may need to add small amounts of water to ensure the rice is fully cooked. Only had a spoonful of water at a time to prevent excess moisture.

# Best Pesto

If you love pesto, you'll know that there's nothing better than pesto that's homemade! If you are growing your own basil, this is a great way to use it during growing season.

Ingredients:
2 or 3 handfuls of fresh basil
1/4 cup of olive oil

2 tablespoons of toasted pine nuts ("toast" your raw pine nuts by heating in a dry pan)
1 centimetre cube of parmesan cheese
1/2 clove of garlic
salt and pepper to taste

Method:
Blitz all ingredients in a food processor. Taste and add salt if necessary. Increase the olive oil to your individual taste too! Use this on pasta, bruschetta, or as a flavour enhancer for or other Italian cooking or hummus. Alternatively, increase the amount of olive oil and store in a tall, lidded jar to use as a dip for breads and crackers.

# 30 Second Salad Dressing

Ingredients:
1/4 cup olive or walnut oil
1 or 2 tablespoons of white wine or white balsamic vinegar
1/2 teaspoon of wholegrain or dijon mustard
a pinch of salt
a pinch of pepper
1/4 clove of minced garlic (optional)

Method:
Pour all ingredients in a jar, cover and shake.

# Final Thoughts

Throughout this book you've learned that your kitchen doesn't need to be untidy just because it's the busiest room in the house! There are tons of things you can do to keep your countertops sleek and your cupboards organized! Remember to keep anything you can reuse and get rid of the stuff you no longer need. Be ruthless with your belongings if you have a tendency to hoard. Don't forget to keep everything labeled to ensure the whole family is onboard. In order to save money, make sure you're shopping smart! Make more foods from scratch, and make your own household cleaners!

The most important thing to remember where your kitchen needs are concerned is to think outside the box! Ask your friends and relatives for tips and recipes and have fun turning your family kitchen into the savvy kitchen of your dreams! Oh! And don't forget to plan something fun to do with all the money you save!